Introduction

The primary purpose of this book is to capture the essence of what Cowboyist Party stands for. I wish for this to be a clear and concise piece, written with the intention of providing a practical and straightforward look at what the Cowboyist Party, my party, stands for.

I have begun to form a concrete set of principles, values and ideas which will be the foundation of this new organization. Currently, my main focus is not to politically organize any group of individuals for the purpose of lobbying or winning elections. Instead, my objective is to craft an intellectual base for the Cowboyist ideology and, by extension, the party. It is my goal here to outline the fundamentals of "Cowboyist thought."

This leaves us with a much bigger question: What do I ultimately hope to accomplish by the foundation of this party? To put it simply: It is not my aim to reign supreme on the political stage or take the majority of the votes. I don't believe that American third parties will ever possess political clout equal to, or even approaching, either main party. My ultimate goal is to gather like-minded individuals, to influence *people*, not elections. The Cowboyist Party may be a political organization which eventually nominates candidates to fill seats but that is not, *and never will be*, its main purpose. The Cowboyist Party seeks to create a new metapolitical movement and bring said movement into the public eye. I want to present an alternative to those seeking one. I want to move beyond the battlefield of ballot boxes and into the realm of ideas, actions, thoughts, motivations and purpose. I want life to be about more than dollars and cents, more than statutes and bills. I want to urge the creation of a new way of life for the modern man, one that will secure his self-reliance and strength. I want to put forth a vision which will unify and strengthen each individual who holds true to it.

The Cowboyist Party is not partisan and will avoid, until it becomes a necessary part of our political position, the propagandizing which nearly always walks hand-in-hand with political movements. I do not believe it is the Cowboyist Party's place to further the partisan divide in this country. I do believe that it is in our interest to propose workable, long-term solutions which will provide both personal and national success.

Brief Summary of the Cowboyist Party

The Cowboyist Party is a movement dedicated to the creation of a new mentality. This party represents an idea. It is not a strictly political entity. It is not a centralized political apparatus like the Democratic Party or the Republican Party. It represents something much more: The dissatisfaction felt by millions of Americans; the realization that the political game, while it can still be played with some success, should not be our only priority; the concept of inner development. I am opposed to technocracy and to the capitalist interpretation of life only as a means to profit and dollars. I am also opposed to the money-prioritizing ideologies of socialism, communism and all their derivatives. The Cowboyist Party seeks to bring to the table a new set of convictions for a new man, a man that is to be forged by his own self-determination and a will for independence.

Why "Cowboyist?"

The name "Cowboyist Party" does seem silly, don't you think? Why does the name seem silly? Because it is. Does that matter? Not really. Do I need to say more?

The name "Cowboyist" conveys a sense of homeliness and community, two of the most precious elements of this party's beliefs. This party is grassroots through and through. This party is very much the kind to knock on your door, ask politely to come in, then sit hearthside with you, listening to your grievances. It is in this spirit of small-town friendship, perhaps even family, that the Cowboyist Party's members may seek election in the future. Although, as has been stated before, politicking is not the primary purpose of the Cowboyist Party, and will take a back seat to the personal growth of party members and the party's ideology.

The Cowboyist Party: Right or Left?

The Cowboyist Party is neither right nor left. I believe that the modern political dichotomy is tired, antiquated and old. Ideally this dichotomy would be retired, but its present strength prevents any third party from making meaningful political progress. The only result of the struggle between the mostly made-up "right" and "left" is dogmatism and the oversimplification of questions crucial to our survival. Political elitism, the product of our deeply rooted two-party system, holds no importance for the average American.

The Cowboyist Party believes not in party lines, but in forward-thinking and personality-driven change. All your questions regarding specific policy may be directed to @officialcowboyistparty on Instagram. Please be aware that not all issues facing us today have been studied by the CBP, and that this party, just like any person or entity, is continually growing and learning. It should also be known that this work is not analytical. It is editorialized, based upon my opinions and is meant to lay out a party platform (of sorts). Discern what you will from the following work, but know that the CBP's official allegiances lie with neither the right nor the left.

The Cowboyist's Oath

I pledge my heart and hands to the pursuit of American principles and freedom. I will do no harm, unless in defense of liberty, posterity and family I am forced to take up arms. I promise to help all those in need, and to work for the betterment of both my neighbors and myself. Duty, fraternity, selflessness; for these I strive, together with all those who will join me.

On Identity

The issues of identity is a pressing one. Firstly, I wish to lay some ground rules pertaining to the Cowboyist Party's conception of identity. It would be unhealthy to sever any person's link to their ancestry, which is partially based on race, as it provides them with both foundation and inspiration. The idea that it is morally wrong to separate a person from his heritage plays a prominent role in our doctrine.

I believe it is obvious that we should work towards creating equity in living conditions between the races. However, I believe that we ought to work towards this goal without any of the connotations of guilt or victimhood commonly associated with such an equalizing process. The drive towards equity is not to be motivated by a feeling of guilt and resultant obligation, but should instead be motivated by the plain and simple fact that racial tensions are in need of defusing. It is the goal of the Cowboyist Party to reach tenable long-term solutions, not to appeal to partisanship and dogmatism.

We are and always will be IN FAVOR of racial identity and heritage, but are also IN

FAVOR of recognizing racial differences in the spirit of reconciliation and co-existence. The United States and similar Western and European nations should retain their European identities. All other nations should maintain their current identities lest they choose to change them. This does not mean that culturally preservationist nations should act with ill-intent towards the rest of the world when there is no reason to do so. Differences, and the acceptance of them, do not necessarily mean conflict, and I believe that understanding this is key to the race issue today.

Our doctrine rests primarily on the realization that any people must have ample space to express elements of culture. The close proximity of differing cultures to one another only provokes conflict, both direct and indirect. The assimilation of all the cultures living together in one nation into one, overarching identity only destroys the diversity it many times claims to protect.

Let's add a personal touch to this argument: Imagine you are put in this situation: You are forced to hang around other individuals who are not only different from you, but are opposed to whatever it is that you enjoy. Imagine that, at best, your neighbors are indifferent to your personal practices. Occasionally, they berate you for your past actions and claim that you must share with them the fruits of your labor. You are begrudgingly forced to comply, otherwise your neighbors look down upon you. Doesn't sound quite so fulfilling, does it? Populations must have room to express their culture, just as individuals must have room to express their personality. Suppressing either will inevitably lead to harmful acting out, similar to how inmates in solitary confinement will resort to cutting themselves as a form of self-expression.

Thus it becomes clear to us that to restrain identity which is based on heritage of any type is wrong. The blossoming of culture rests first on a healthy sense of pride, something which cannot exist in an environment hostile to the very concept of culture. The Cowboyist answer to the question of identity is a positive one. It is nobody's place to deny a person his heritage or his history, especially not in an arbitrary manner.

If one group must give up their identity, then it must be the duty of all others to follow suit. To neuter one animal but not the other not only screams "injustice!", but is also a key ingredient for resentment. The average man will realize what is happening and feel persecuted. Feeling this way, some will lash out. Still more will become fringe, angry and unsociable. It is far safer to advocate for the free and open expression of heritage and history than it is to suppress it. This goes for all groups of people and applies to all elements of culture, even those which may appear ugly.

This does open up one very important question: *What about the United States?* It is the position of the Cowboyist Party that the United States is, in character and culture, a mostly European nation. The population of the United States has been overwhelmingly European for all of its history, and this only began to change in the last fifty years. It is unjust to allow the whole world into the United States as if everyone on this planet has a claim to its soil and resources. We should recognize that the United States is now an established nation and that its identity should no longer be in flux. The United States has never been without an established, dominant culture, and it is wrong in many ways to say that the European-Americans residing here have failed to create a culture of their own. We do not debate the legitimacy of Mexico's culture; everyone acknowledges that there are things which are Mexican, and that the Mexicans should have the right to preserve those things, among which is their demographic majority within Mexico. I believe the same rule ought to be applied to European-Americans in the United States. This should not bring resentment, nor should it bring conflict. This realization should not be difficult. *It should be regarded as a fact of life that some nations are a certain way, and do not stand to gain anything by changing.* This is not to say that European-American society is perfect or ever has been. Rather, my point here is that the demographic destruction of European-Americans is unjustified and should be opposed.

Immigration, the movement of large populations between locations, is a complicated business. Its effects are rippling. They don't end, they only become less and less significant over time (assuming immigrant communities assimilate). This is why I believe that we should remain skeptical of mass-immigration especially. We cannot assume that by simply importing massive amounts of people into the United States we are accomplishing anything of worth. What will that get us? A higher population? Most definitely. A marginal increase in GDP? Maybe, but so what? There will still exist nations like Mexico and Honduras and Guatemala, places where crime is an epidemic and poverty is the rule. By moving their people here we will only succeed in duplicating their nations' abysmal conditions within our own borders. Instead, we ought to consider options which will ensure other nations' future prosperity. We must make it possible for the migrants at our southern border to make a prosperous life in their own nations, and to see them rise above crime and poverty. No moment would be greater in the history of Latin America than the moment when countries like Honduras and Guatemala could boast a low crime rate, high employment, quality infrastructure and educational systems, and a political apparatus which runs efficiently and with minimum corruption. These developments will doubtless require massive effort (and certainly the aid of the American people), but will be worth far more, in the long run, than a simple relocation of those nations' populations to America. There is no good reason to disrupt life in the United States if it is possible to help these people create their own prosperous nations. No mission that I could undertake outside of the United States is more important to me than this: the creation of safe and prosperous communities in nations traditionally plagued by poverty and crime.

On Ecology

"The most central and irrational faith among people is the faith in technology and economical growth. Its priests believe until their death that material prosperity bring enjoyment and happiness—even though all the proofs in history have shown that only lack and attempt cause a life worth living, that the material prosperity doesn't bring anything else than despair."

~ Pentti Linkola

The preservation of the world's natural resources ranks high on the Cowboyist Party's list of priorities. The cultivation of a sense of connection between our earth and everyday people would be the most effective form of ecological preservation. By tying people and nature together we can bring into popular culture a healthy respect for nature's beauty and complexity. This proposition brings to the forefront an obvious social contradiction: Money versus ecology. While the growth of human economies continues, and not only at the expense of non-human nature but also essential human characteristics, we observe that the natural world is becoming increasingly disturbed by our development. In many ways this problem is one had by individuals, not only by human society at large. We, both as personalities and as a people, must learn to coexist with nature.

It is preferable to interpret the ongoing environmental crisis as one which is solvable through mostly moderate means. It is not a very palatable thought that civilization is entirely incompatible with the natural world, especially because civilization is the inevitable result of humanity's (or any intelligent life, as a matter of fact) existence. It is because of this that the Cowboyist Party advocates for both adjustments in macro-social trends, such as corporate attitudes towards pollution, and in micro-social trends, such as the average person's connection to nature. We must do everything in our power to get people out into the woods. With the proper education, the average American could become an avid naturalist and preservationist. Of course we must also temper ourselves; too many tourists will inevitably disrupt and abuse popular, beautiful ecosystems.

A theme which will recur in this work is the prioritization of ideas and non-economical issues over money. This is a key tenet of the

Cowboyist Party, and is based on the realization that the modern money-economy is just that: *Modern*. Humanity has gone without such an economy for most of its history and suffered little for it. It is not we who need Amazon, Google or online banking; it is these things that need us. Their well-being should not be placed above that of the American people. This will be discussed in more detail later.

In an ideal world, it would be possible for all technology and industry to work in harmony with both humanity's economic and physical needs as well as nature's need for independence from civilization. In a perfect world, humanity would not use technology in a gluttonous fashion, as we do now, but would restrain ourselves in order to better protect the natural world. Perhaps in the future this paradise-esque vision of human-nature interaction will be proven to be only a pipe dream; humanity may be too selfish, *and above all uncoordinated*, to accomplish such a monumental task as this. It remains to be seen just how destructive human actions have been, and many climate alarmists only distort the picture further. It is my hope that the Cowboyist Party's brand of optimism will be proven right over the coming decades and centuries. If it is not, then we can expect that all other issues will appear very small compared to the environmental havoc wrought by millennia of human expansion and domination over non-human nature. From the possibility of environmental collapse comes the Cowboyist Party's emphasis on disaster preparedness and individual or small community-based self-sufficiency.

The Cowboyist Party's attitude towards human-nature relations rests on the idea that humans, while exhibiting sophisticated behaviors as well as sentience, should still be counted among animals. It is not our place to be above or below nature, but instead to be among it.

If the state of our environment is not as dismal as many alarmists make it out to be, then we are left with more room to act with moderate steps. Along with this it will be necessary to change the way we think of human-nature relations. Specifically, we must begin to view ourselves as only one part of the natural world rather than as something which is above or outside it. We must take efforts to curb consumerist culture if we are to go on living in a world populated by upwards of seven billion people. The sorts of modern lifestyles we in the West live, and increasingly in other parts of the world, are not compatible with the long-term sustainability of either civilization or nature. We must adapt our civilization to suit nature, not the other way around. We have been making changes to nature in order to build civilization for centuries. These have nearly always been absorbed by nature due to their relatively small impact on the environment, but with the advent of modern, industrial technologies we now have the potential to outgrow the earth's ability to sustain us. With a great amount of effort, a mild solution to this problem could be successful. However it is inadvisable, in the event that the climate situation is as bad as it has been made out to be, to have great faith that any plan to counteract ecological collapse will or could ever be executed. The coordination between governments that would be required is likely too great, with too many other issues getting in the way of successful cooperation between most world leaders. Our greatest tool for addressing the climate issue is local education. Young people in all places should learn about the environment, animal and plant species, and other similar things. The young should connect with nature via hikes, camping trips and other outdoor activities. These things, coupled with a spirit of respect for nature, will serve us better than any pen-and-paper policy could ever hope to.

The Cowboyist Party will always maintain an optimistic outlook on the question of climate change (nature is incredibly resilient, it has always rebounded from even catastrophic losses). However, in the long run, we do not dare to compare human lives to the health of our whole planet. These two things are not the same and do not hold the same value. Our world sustains many millions more species that our own, and we should not act selfishly when it comes to ecology. The planet's well-being is worth protecting at any given opportunity. Especially when compared to economic growth, which usually does not stand directly opposed to environmental interests, the health of our planet is infinitely more important.

I believe we must also acknowledge that the Industrial Revolution and consequential developments in technology have resulted in a social spirit permeated in monetized values. This has brought an unnatural, money-driven hue to our societies. The Industrial Revolution has brought the destruction of animal habitats, the rise of both classism and socialism, and explosions in greed and pettiness which defy quantification. While extravagant wealth has been created, especially when compared to the wealth (or lack thereof) of our ancestors, I cannot help but feel that it is decadent and far from being worth its cost. What is the chance that the average man will become a millionaire or a billionaire? Slim to none, *but mostly none*. Why is it that we obsess over wages and amounts of money when we live in a world which is more than capable of providing enough of those things to make everyone's life bearable? It is because that is the nature of large systems of capital. Communism, capitalism, socialism; they are all the same. They all cry for money, better wages, better benefits, but never for an end to the capital system of artificial scarcity, the system which has brought misery to people all over the world. While the Industrial Revolution has brought us prosperity in the short-term, and some additional creature comforts, I do not believe it has been, overall and taking into account both history and the future, beneficial to the human race.

The Cowboyist solution to this problem is not to destroy the capital system, but to advocate for the *avoidance* of it. People who choose to take on a lifestyle of self-sufficiency will be those who are the most successful in beating today's consumer society. This is not a society-wide solution, but is instead one which will have to be implemented on a personal basis. Again the Cowboyist maxim of fraternity applies; It will be personal connections and friends who revolt against the modern world, not all of society. For those who cannot or will not avoid capital society, I can only recommend that you attempt to close the ever-increasing wealth and wage gap between the rich and poor. If this is not fixed, we shall see unrest and comparative poverty unlike any seen before in human history.

I believe we should also see clearly that the Industrial Revolution and its derivatives have produced living and working conditions which are in some cases downright dystopian. Recent advancements in surveillance technology as well as increasingly strict social standards regarding "politically correct" behaviors have reduced the amount of freedom possessed by the average man. We no longer live in a society in which there are moments of disconnectedness: *pure freedom.* Before advanced communications technology and the "video cameras on every corner" phenomenon, it was possible for people to act however they wanted, so long as no one got hurt. Today, it is nearly impossible for anyone to act the way they wish to, unless the way they act is deemed to be harmless or is approved of by those in charge. Ever said something controversial on social media? Congratulations, you've just been fired! Maybe you dawdled a bit at work today? Well, no worries, Amazon's got you covered! They know exactly when you're slacking off, all thanks to a wonderful movement-measuring bracelet they invented. Even controversial memes can get you no-knocked by the FBI. We truly do live in a *free* society!

One goal of this party is to alleviate this inhuman pressure, to force big tech to take a massive step back. They, the Bezos and Zuckerbergs of the world, will doubtless be our biggest opponents if the CBP ever becomes a national party. The Cowboyist Party aims to bring an end to their stupidly totalitarian methods of control, be they those found on the warehouse floor or on social media. Freedom to speak your mind and freedom to do honest work unmolested are both freedoms the Cowboyist Party seeks to protect at all costs. If that takes a decrease in GDP or worker productivity, or digs into the profits of men like Jeff Bezos and Mark Zuckerberg, *so be it*. They don't care about the average man, and they won't until it suits their own interests. In fact, I believe we find that the proof is in the pudding when it comes to this claim. After all, this book was published using Amazon's self-publishing system. If Amazon is willing to make money off of a book written by someone who despises them, their business practices, and their very existence, what *won't* they make money off of? (I make exactly $0.24 off each sale of *The Cowboyist Proclamation*. Of the total price tag, $3.99, I see *twenty-four cents*.)

Here is just one example, among many, of how technology has grown to become more of a burden than a boon. Amazon recently received a patent for wristbands which would allow them to *track the hand movements* of their employees. The system that would accompany these bracelets involves ultrasonic devices (be placed around any Amazon workplace), the bracelets themselves, and a central module designed to manage the measurements recorded by the bracelets. If the worker moves the wrong item the bracelet will buzz. Too many errors and the worker will be fired. Amazon has a long history of creating inhumane working conditions. They have repeatedly been accused of timing their employees' bathroom breaks, making some work weeks of up to fifty-five hours, and timing them while they pack boxes to ensure they meet

Amazon's standards of efficiecy. If Amazon workers fail to meet the standards set by their employers they will be fired. These so-called "productivity firings" plague Amazon warehouses, with just one location firing hundreds of employees for reasons relating to productivity between August, 2017 and September, 2018. Amazon even tracks what it calls "time off task" (abbreviated as TOT, using the company's language), and employees can be fired if they take too long in between scanning packages.

Do not dare to tell me that these things are natural, or that they are conducive to a person's humanity. These conditions are cruel, stressful, and indicative of a wider trend within our society: the tendency to value profit over human value. While this is indeed a well-known and cliche saying, it bears repeating again. The worst part of this reality is that it is the logical conclusion of the rights-based system our society has been built around. Businesses are afforded the right to do this and that, and to impose restrictions and harsh conditions on their workers because the property is *theirs*. While this is true to a certain degree, this idea is undeniably favorable to overzealous privatization and exploitation. A great part of the power that some businesses are given finds its origin in the legal system, which is frequently abused by companies such as Facebook and Amazon. Corporations are considered to be people (when they certainly aren't), which results in their being able to claim rights which shouldn't be given to organizations or financial entities.

Many will attempt to address the issues of monetization, mass-consumption and over-technologization by providing solutions based on the technology which brought us to these situations. I believe that this is a fundamentally flawed approach. If we continue to utilize the same technologies which led us to our current position, will we not end up at the same point we started? There is a need for something more, something radical, which will shake up the technological scene, perhaps even leave it behind. If this can be done even on an individual level, one person at a time, we will be making progress.

SLEEP OUTSIDE. TAKE LONG HIKES. MAKE A BEDROLL. BUY A LEVER GUN. COOK OVER AN OPEN FIRE. BUILD A CABIN. GROW A GARDEN. LEARN SURVIVAL SKILLS. **BE A MODERN COWBOY.**

On Personality

The importance of true personality for a functioning society is greatly underestimated in the modern day. This matter is not one which centers around one person in some sort of Messianic cult, rather it is centered around the realization that in order to create a quality society, there must be quality people within it. The journey towards excellence is primarily a matter of heart. For those who have no qualms with struggle, and even see it as an essential element of life, there is no barrier but the physical. It is our problem today that many individuals are not motivated, they do not look at the world around them and think to themselves, "This could be better." There are many who are roped up in trivial concerns (trivial on the large scale, not necessarily to the person in question) which have little to no bearing on humanity's future. They see and feel no reason to improve themselves in pursuit of a greater ideal. The soul-crushing nature of today's society is chiefly responsible for this, in my opinion. The adoption of philosophy which abstracts human experiences and "rationalizes" them has been the downfall of personality and true personhood. We must work to counteract this by regaining lost mythologies and legends. We must allow ourselves to romanticize and to develop positive historical narratives that provide us with inspiration and foundation.

The Cowboyist Party believes in a resurgence of personality in the form of a conception which emphasizes community, spirit and motivation. There must be beliefs higher than those pertaining to small problems, and beliefs which go beyond mere humanity. It is the place of personality to provide motivation and satisfaction. These sensations should not be looked for in material gain or possessions except in a very few cases, perhaps when dealing with an important family heirloom or another item which holds great sentimental value. These things should be sought out inside of your own self or in the form of a higher goal or cause, such as a community, movement or ideal. It should be encouraged for people to explore their own motivations and to give meaning to their actions. For Cowboyist Party members, motivation exists outside and above modernity. We reject the spirit of modernity and all its reductionist ideas. Spiritual and religious practices are not to be minimized in favor of science and rationale. *Man is not a means to a material end and not one person should be treated as if that is all they are.* What is to be done in a general sense, on the large-scale? The state of modern society is such that attempting to save its entirety would be impossible. Thus we of the Cowboyist Party turn our eyes to personality. In the absence of a means toward wider social change, we must pursue personal developments. The practical path towards the cultivation of worthy, virtuous personalities is a long one. The goal here is to create a class of men which can simultaneously exist within and without the modern world. With this goal in mind, the CBP believes that we ought to work to develop a nearly anarchistic personality, revolting against the modern world and all its veneers at any given opportunity. This is why we latch onto the symbolism of the cowboy, the pioneer and the minuteman; we are free men of virtue and self-discipline. We aim to be the modern bandit, the cultured thug, anything but an advocate for the bourgeois, capital-driven society of today. We aim for a new man of family, freedom and fraternity with all those who will reciprocate it.

We will not be bandits and thugs in the literal sense, of course. The essential idea is that one should at the same time be well-read, articulate and intelligent, but unafraid of physical tasks, self-sufficiency and self-defense. In that context those phrases should be looked at with an air of opposition to society, meaning that we are self-sufficient in spite of or in opposition to society's condition.

As a remedy to the world's lack of personality the Cowboyist Party offers the metaphysic of the cowboy. The metaphysic of the cowboy has played an important role in developing the American spirit. Before the cowboy there was the pioneer, the pilgrim, and the minuteman. All were examples of the American lust for exploration, conquest and independence. All these things came together to create the ideal of the homestead. We still observe this idea today, although struggling, in the American Dream. While ideas about what makes up the American Dream have been changing in recent times, I do not believe this flux should stand in the way of our claims to the ideal of the homestead. Every man ought to own a home, be able to support a family, to defend himself, and be self-reliant in as many ways as possible. The metaphysic of the cowboy is simply a different way of expressing the quintessential American quality that is *independence*.

How does this relate to our situation today, and what lessons are to be taken from this "metaphysic of the cowboy?" American society today reflects much of what independent men such as cowboys, pioneers, and minutemen likely would have thought unnecessary or weak. While societies all around the world, and their ideas about a myriad of topics, have changed drastically in the last two centuries, the image of the pioneer ought to remain an admirable one. As American society grows increasingly interwoven, and people become increasingly dependent upon one another for services which guarantee their quality of life, we drift further and further away from the ideal of the homestead. There was a brief period from the late 1940s to the mid-1970s in which a man could provide for his family by working a run-of-the-mill job. The United States had no shortage of factory jobs, cheap education with which to acquire said jobs, and cheap land, homes, and other familial necessities. To attend college now costs an arm and a leg, jobs are far from guaranteed, and the costs of essentials like housing, medical care, even groceries, have skyrocketed. Standard of living and access to luxuries like television, smart phones, and computers has increased drastically, but our independence and individual/familial autarchy has withered. This is where we find the problem.

Increases in standards of living are well and good, but where do we find the time to think of our *standards of civilization*? Along with this increased standard of living have come diversions, vices, and restrictions. The average American now has access to endless entertainment and sexual stimulation (be it through explicit pornography or the softcore porn of modern fashion and celebrity-media). Young men find themselves to be increasingly socially isolated and sexually denied or frustrated (see: the "incel" crisis), not to mention alienated by an increasingly feminized society that has no room for traditional manhood. In this restricted society there is no tolerance for manhood. Men require breathing space, the danger of exploration, and experiences which bring to light their nature. The metaphysic of the cowboy provides all these antidotes, and will help to bring meaning to the lives of today's rootless young men.

Through self-reliance we will build our new man. The goal of this new man will be to distance himself as much as he can from the flashing lights of modern society and its frivolity. The illnesses forced on to men by modern culture and its endless stimulation, consumerism, sex, drugs and fame are plagues which many have yet to recognize. I hope that we will see the dangers presented by these new addictions before it is too late, before there is too little manhood left in us to be salvaged.

Men have found themselves ravaged by this new society, and it is clear to many (including myself) that our current situation could become unworkable. Just between 2010 and 2013, those American men who were prescribed testosterone-boosting medications increased by double. Things like this have a myriad of causes, in my opinion, ranging from increasingly poor food quality to an increase in feminine social pressures in the lives of young men and boys. A study published in the *Journal of Clinical Endocrinology and Metabolism* in 2007 found an average drop in male testosterone levels by one percent annually since the 1980s. Testosterone levels have been decreasing since even before the

1980s. A Danish study found that men born in the 1960s had fourteen percent less testosterone than men born in the 1920s, just forty-odd years earlier. This should be an obvious signal to society that we're in trouble. Imagine the outcry if in one generation women lost fourteen percent of their estrogen. Whether these changes are wholly socially conditioned (in that they are being caused by the widespread disapproval with which masculinity is now met), or they are a natural response to the sedentary lifestyle now being lived by many American (and Western) men is up to you to decide. Either way, this data, and other data like it, proves that modernity and changing gender roles are wreaking havoc on manhood (and womanhood, but with the consent of women, who I suspect see their feminine natures as being inadequate).

Because of this we must attempt to separate ourselves from the social mores which tear down traditional manhood in an attempt to revise it. The point of separating yourself from society's norms is not to attempt to improve society—in most ways it is too far gone to be changed much for the better—but instead to exist outside of its trends. This is our only prayer of maintaining a life which could be called "healthy."

On God

It is my position that the existence of something "higher" than humanity is certain. There simply cannot be, in my opinion, *only humanity*. Even if there is no "God" in the traditional sense, meaning that He is an independent actor who makes decisions and holds supreme power, like the ultimate king, then there must be some *higher idea*. This higher idea will doubtless differ from person to person. For me, it is the sense of continuity that comes with history. History, to me, is like a river; all is connected. We embody, in the present, both the events of the past and the potential of the future. Our present is one link in an ever-lengthening chain of personalities, events, ideas and mishaps. In this I find meaning. The past gives me a certain kind of drive, a motivation. To think that I am the product of millennia of marriage, childbirth, coincidence and happenstance is awe-inspiring. It does not fill me with dread that my existence is only one of many eventualities. Instead, it brings over me a feeling of responsibility. I have been given one life, by the grace of historical chance, and because I am so blessed I must live this one life in a way which would inspire pride amongst the greatest figures in humanity's history.

There really is not much for me to say on the issue of God. Not much can be said by me because while I am a spiritual person, I do not enjoy sharing those beliefs with many people. The spiritual and religious beliefs of humans are vast and differ too much to allow for me to weigh in one them without becoming very knowledgeable on those topics. It is more comfortable for me to keep these beliefs to myself. However, I will make one recommendation to those seeking spiritual advice: Do not go without spirituality of some kind. To believe that there is nothing above humanity will drag you down into despondency. There must be something, *anything*, that you prize above everyday life and will continue to provide you fulfillment. I recommend that this be an idea, a family or community, or a struggle you deem worthwhile. *Do not throw meaning out the window because of a ridiculous obsession with proving you can exist without it.*

The Right to Bear Arms

The question of firearm ownership is needlessly complicated today. The Cowboyist Party believes that so long as a man does not commit a crime with a firearm, he should be allowed to own whatever firearm(s) he pleases. This is not only for the benefit of the individual conscientious citizen, but it is for the benefit of the common defense of our American nation. The right to self-defense is inalienable, and to take away the capacity of a man to defend his home, convictions and livelihood would be paramount to murder. For much of America's history the local militia played an integral role in the defense of our nation from enemies both foreign and domestic. In almost every conflict from our founding until the Spanish-American War, local militias fought proudly alongside federal troops. The right of individuals to found and officiate a militia should be upheld without compromise, as should their right to own whatever firearm they deem as being necessary to both the common and personal defense.

The firearm is a manifestation of the liberty which both America and the Cowboyist Party hold so dear. A firearm symbolizes independence, self-reliance and the taming of wilderness. Since we stand in opposition to the typification of people and rampant capitalism, it makes sense that we should advocate for the free and open formation of citizen-militias, particularly those with goals relating to the formation of independent communities of exceptional individuals dedicated to preserving traditional American freedom. These liberty-oriented militias and persons will be integral in the creation of a renewed American spirit, destined to create a United States, nay, a world, where men may again live freely.

Miscellaneous Cowboyist Writings

The Cowboy-Anarch Archetype

The state of modern society is such that attempting to save its entirety would be impossible. Thus we of the Cowboyist Party turn our eyes to personality. In the absence of a means toward wider social change, we must pursue personal developments. The practical path towards the cultivation of worthy, virtuous personalities is a long one. The goal here is to create a class of men which can simultaneously exist within and without the modern world. With this goal in mind, the CBP believes that we ought to work to develop a nearly anarchistic personality, revolting against the modern world and all its veneers at any given opportunity. This is why we latch onto the symbolism of the cowboy, the pioneer and the minuteman; we are free men of virtue and self-discipline. We aim to be the modern bandit, the cultured thug, anything but an advocate for the bourgeois, capital-driven society of today. We aim for a new man of family, freedom and fraternity with all those who will reciprocate it.

I recommend reading Julius Evola's essay "The Youth, The Beats and Right-Wing Anarchists" if you have any further questions regarding this.

The Indian's Impact Today

Today the American Indian is remembered as a defeated man, a victim of the cold and unforgiving white settler. The Indian civilizations of plains, hills, forests and deserts—speaking a thousand tongues belonging to as many linguistic groups—are long gone. Yet the ideal of the Indian lives on in popular culture, albeit in a distorted, incorrect way. Today I feel that the philosophy of Indians should be investigated, possibly even co-opted, by factions seeking to distance themselves from modern industrial-capital society.

There are many Indian tribes, so many in fact that to attempt to represent all their Traditions without a long, in-depth series of books would do them no justice. Therefore I will stick to generalities, and by no means claim to hold comprehensive knowledge of these subjects.

The Indian philosophies stand in contrast to the progressive, Western-minded thinking that overran them. The Indian peoples, while seeming too simple and "uncomplicated" to the average Western eye, held profound beliefs regarding the natural world, humanity's place in it, and personal spiritual growth. It is beliefs of these types, with our own beliefs overlaid, that members of the CBP ought to adopt. We should look upon nature with a homely feeling; it is from the earth that all we know was birthed. We make use of the world's resources to live, and do so because we are animals. We ought to live in ways that fulfill ourselves; do not work yourself to death each day. We ought to develop our personalities; live without popular media and celebrity-obsessions, they will give you nothing of meaning.

I encourage you all to delve into the realm of nature. Make use of state and national parks. Bring a notebook hiking, write a passage for your great-grandchildren to read when you are long dead. Study the ancient Traditions of varied peoples. Forget smokestacks, car horns and yellow office lights. Escape from the modern world and live in free air.

Moral Capital

The only reason that society is trending towards equality is because of capitalism. And no, by 'capitalism' I do not mean the sensationalized libertarian and anarcho-capitalist version of 'capitalism.' By 'capitalism' I mean the raw, real means by which capital ('capital' meaning goods, services and finances) is distributed and manufactured throughout the globe. The ever-expanding capitalist economy requires an ever-growing labor pool in order to function. The economy cannot grow unless there are more people willing to help it to do so. This is why we see such a sense of urgency being directed towards equality of all types. Capital sees no difference between black and white, so long as the job gets done. It stands to reason that, in an industrial, capital-driven society, any person who could perform a task that benefits a business or other bulwark of industrial society would be brought into the workforce. This is why women were taken out of the home, why billionaires finance immigration initiatives; Industry wants cheap labor. At some point, industry will finally start looking into whether or not automation is cheaper than hiring droves of low-wage immigrants. Not only will this irrevocably destroy millennia-old social mores, it will destroy (and already has begun to do so) all forms of personality, to say nothing of the cultural genocide (cultural homogenization via consumerism) which has already swept across the world, especially the West, Korea and Japan.

The Cowboyist Party on the Nature of Humans and of Government

Much of the modern political world rests on conclusions made by Enlightenment-era philosophers. These conclusions found that human beings were, by their nature, good. It was advanced by minds such as John Locke that mankind existed, prior to government, in a "state of nature," where no man would ever deprive another of life, liberty or property. Locke thought this because he believed that within this state of nature, which existed without government, all men were equals. No man held a power that every other man did not also hold. To put it simply: It wasn't that some people had guns while others didn't, rather it was a world in which either everyone had a gun or no one did. It is ideas like these that today's political thinking is based upon.

The Cowboyist Party thinks differently, and instead advances a theory of realpolitik. It is my opinion that government's development is the result of interplay between state entities throughout all of history. While Locke's theory states that government was formed by "the people" in order to protect their natural rights and liberty, my theory is that governments formed via natural processes of Power accumulation. Here's an example: The first governments were of a tribal nature. Usually small in size, these societies were usually ruled by either a single person or a small group of persons. To begin, these tribes were mere bands numbering not more than two dozen. Eventually, through decades or even centuries of conflict, one band became large enough to call itself a tribe, and all along this journey to tribalism was continually gaining Power with which to govern. This same rule applies to all forms of government throughout history. As societies and cultures clashed, some won out over others and became more Powerful. We can witness the same principle of Power at work in most governments, where agencies, individual actors and departments are vying for Power.

Therefore it is not the people who are responsible for the creation of government, rather it is the government which is responsible for its own perpetuation.

The reason I capitalize Power is because in this case I am using it as a measure of 'real Power.' This includes things such as the physical ability for a government or ruler to enforce their laws, their ability to coerce citizens into following laws without violence, and their ability to punish lawbreakers. More or less, Power is the core of government, and anyone who seeks to govern must accumulate or usurp Power.

Cowboyism: Theory vs. Praxis

The Cowboyist Party is of course at this point a mostly theoretical movement. If we wish to turn the CBP into a practical, even revolutionary movement, then we must focus our attention on several matters of praxis. Praxis is the translation of theory into practical action, and is a crucial step in any process of social change.

What is the CBP's praxis? To answer this question we must first pick a clear and concise objective, towards which we can strive without confusion. This is by far the most difficult part of praxis, as there are many issues of import facing us today. I believe the chief concerns of the CBP can be narrowed down to three things: Immigration reform, gun control, and censorship, especially that which is propagated or enforced by big tech. I am a staunch proponent of security-minded immigration policy, but I believe that that has now become the general trend in politics. Gun control is a different matter, and regarding that topic I find myself firmly against the regulation of firearms. However, there are already many prominent organizations dedicated to fighting against the Second Amendment's opponents (the GOA, FPC). It is in this third realm that the CBP finds its practical purpose. It should be our main goal to call out and defeat big tech's encroachments on human privacy.

We will focus on issues of technology-based censorship and some of its ancillaries. These will include the rigging of search results on web browsers, the media's ridiculous bias, and journalism's rabid tendencies. We will also oppose Facebook, Google and Amazon's efforts to track or regulate human behavior. Anytime you see a piece of media about these companies and their efforts to restrict human freedom, let it be known that you disagree. For now there is next to nothing we can do in terms of real action to fight these gigantic companies, besides cause chaos and make a splash in public discourse.

The main goal of the CBP is to remove modern technology's privacy-ending yoke from the shoulders of man.

The American Labor Theory of Value

American liberty is based upon independence. This independence comes in many forms, but pertains chiefly to the concept of individual/familial autarky. The American man was a craftsman, a skilled artisan who worked honorably at his trade to support his family. He owned his means of production, and was the first to receive profits from his products or services. The American industrial revolution changed all this, and caused the American economy to undergo vast changes. The most influential, and frustrating, change brought on by the industrial revolution is the practice of wage labor.

Wage labor when it was first introduced to America in the 1830s and 1840s was viewed by some as paramount to slavery. If you were a wage worker you were in the service of another person, a person who you depended upon for your livelihood. This created a relationship of dependency between the employee, who had no say in how his workplace was run, and the employer. You were, all of a sudden, bound inseparably to the well-being of a larger economy and therefore unable to remain fully independent and free. The industrial system restricted the freedom of formerly independent artisans and craftsmen. Local businesses could not compete with the low prices of industrially-manufactured goods and were forced to close. The local craftsmen were subdued by larger companies, who could hire many unskilled workers to complete the same tasks that one highly skilled artisan would otherwise. The development of American capitalism via industrialization killed the Founders' American Dream wherein every man would be able to secure a livelihood for himself through self-enterprising artisanship or agrarianism.

The reality of wage labor forces us to realize the following: No matter how free and independent we may think we are, there is no true freedom within any variety of industrial society, be it capitalist, communist or anything in between. If you need to ask permission or be approved of by an external entity in order to make a living, you are not free.

The Metaphysic of the Cowboy, the American's Relationship to Nature, and Spiritual Development

There isn't much value placed in the spirit today. This is due in part, I believe, to the near complete destruction of organized religion in the modern Western world. But still the importance of spiritual beliefs and experiences holds out against secularism, even if only by a thread. In our post-religious world ("religious" as in organized religion) the importance of individual spiritual and religious development has increased tenfold. Cowboyist doctrine provides us with some methods of pursuing spiritual development which together have synthesized a unique brand of spiritualism: the Metaphysic of the Cowboy. Of course this idea will have a sort of modern hue to it, given the historical circumstances it was conceived in.

The Metaphysic of the Cowboy has been discussed by me before, most notably in posts on this account and as published in The Cowboyist Proclamation. To give a brief summary: The Metaphysic of the Cowboy is one which emphasizes stoicism, self-discipline and development. In this post I will discuss its spiritual implications.

The greatest spiritual resource for the American Cowboyist will be our nation's incredible natural beauty and resources. This is what I believe gives Americans a totally unique opportunity for spiritual development. In many places in the United States there is access to thousands of acres of public land where hunting and hiking is permitted. Unlike many other nations, like those in the Old World, for example, the United States offers an environment friendly to firearms ownership and to the outdoorsman. Combining these two elements enables a man to experience both nature and self-reliance at the same time, opening the way for a spiritual connection to the land, his ancestors, and America's national mythology.

To immerse oneself in nature is to immerse oneself in your ancestry. While man, through his invention of conveniences and other tools meant to aid in survival of the elements, has distanced himself from nature, our connection to it is a fundamental one.

The American Pioneer Spirit: The First 'American Dream'

The American pioneer is under-appreciated. Their hardships and sacrifices built our nation. Disease, starvation, cold and other similar obstacles claimed the lives of many intrepid settlers. Their journeys Westward were difficult and filled with trials. And yet, to our benefit, they pressed on. I look back on the pioneers, pilgrims, settlers and colonists, among whose ranks I can count many of my ancestors, with pride, respect and gratitude. Our nation would not be as powerful as it is today without the dedication of these millions of settlers, who created themselves thousands of communities and helped establish the American way of life.

The pioneer embodies many traditional American principles: liberty, self-sufficiency, an appreciation and respect for nature, and the ideal of the homestead, just to name a few. In many respects the American pioneer spirit lives on, but in far more ways it has been neutered. Regretfully, the Western frontier has been closed for over a century, and the United States has taken on a new, stagnant and urban character. Especially since the end of the Great War, our government and society have taken greater and greater steps toward the limitation of traditional American social mores and freedoms.

Where there once stood homesteads, wild prairies and forests now sit suburbs. The majority of people now live in cities, unabsorbed by the natural world, their lives forever separated from humanity's primal nature. Very few can say that they experienced the same things their father, grandfather and great-grandfather did. Our way of life has been altered irreparably, and I believe this to be a shame. The least we can do in order to correct this injustice is to remember the wagon trains, the pioneers and their families.

Co-opting Enlightenment Ideals

While it may be philosophically and theoretically correct to dismantle the ideas of the Enlightenment, it is not practical. Instead, propose that we ought to co-opt them, as I believe this to be the best path towards remedying the damage that has been done by them. Since they are immovable due to their thorough application and propagation over the last two hundred years, and have permeated the spirits of each man through and through, it is better to adapt them to our purposes than it is to attempt to destroy and replace them. This requires that the energies of the people must be directed towards constructive pursuits.

I will begin by providing a brief outline of the reasons for my skepticism of Enlightened ideas. These ideas are leading us in dubious directions. In just the last two hundred years we have gone from traditionally arranged, status-conscious marriages to the modern nuclear, two-parent family to the acceptance of nearly any and all relationships regardless of their character. Not only this, but it seems that by and large the family as it used to be has been largely forsaken. These kinds of social change should not be occurring at this pace, if they should occur at all (which is a debate all its own). This incredibly fast-paced social change is unpredictable and uncontrollable by its nature. No one has managed to successfully guide its development as of yet, as the Enlightenment's obsession with crowds has allowed reforms such as these to be passed on a wave of mob support amplified by modern propaganda-media.

What is the alternative? What will stem the tide of torrential "progress?" This is not an easy question to answer, and I believe you will see the reasons for this difficulty quite clearly. Over the last two hundred years the ideas of the Enlightenment have entrenched themselves in the mind of the average person. They have become so potent that each person's worldview is built upon them, unless they have been exposed to traditional (or Traditional, using Evola/Guénon's definitions) modes of thinking through their own research. Ideas descended from the Enlightenment are the default. This requires that we develop our own conclusions, using the already-popular Enlightenment ideas as a base.

I intend to co-opt only the aspects of the Enlightenment which will aid us in constructing an image of man that is hardy, self-disciplined and principled. We will NOT make use of the deconstructionist elements of the Enlightenment which have led to modern movements and ideas such as neoliberalism, nihilism or materialism. My chief goal here is to set out ideas which can be used to hold back the rapid progress of modern civilization. Essentially: We should not place ourselves entirely in opposition to things such as "rights" or the social contract, but should frame them in such a way as to bring about anti-Enlightenment results.

This can be done in any number of ways. In this instance, ideas and conceptions are everything. It is all about getting these ideas into the minds of average people, and propagating them in such a way that they will subtly impact the lives of those who are exposed to them. This is what was done by the first Enlightenment-era philosophers, who first and foremost spread their word to the masses in order to plant a seed of acceptance for their ideas. We should attempt a similar approach, and in many ways already are.

We should advocate specifically for the resurgence of rights pertaining to hardier aspects of society, such as identity, traditions and culture. These things can be adapted to local cultural circumstances. The Cowboyist Party is based in the American midwest, so will reflect the ideals of an American Midwesterner.

The Nature of American Politics and The Modern "Militia Movements"

American politics are distinct. They are distinct not only in the way that they function (practically speaking, with a bicameral legislature, etc.), but also in the way that the purpose of politics is viewed by the American psyche. The average American has never been accustomed to the involvement of government in their everyday life. This has been the rule through even extraordinary times in our history (less so during those times, granted), such as the Civil War or the Great Depression, and it is also the rule in times that are seemingly mundane, like today. If it can be helped, and there is no crisis which seems to need government intervention to be solved, Americans are content to live their lives privately. This mindset has both benefits and detriments, and spills over into the personalities of Americans, cultivating a sense of individuality and independence.

Among the benefits can be numbered the freedoms of enterprise, self-defense and self-determination. These things enable personality to thrive among virtuous peoples, but also enable licentiousness among the non-virtuous. Among the detriments can be counted the decentralization of those virtuous people who would act to uphold the American traditions of self-reliance and community. The latter brings a danger to America: like foxes in a chicken coop, tyrants walk among freemen. And the freemen, not wanting to disturb those who have not yet bothered them, leave them unmolested until they are able to do harm. Then, even after harmful intent on the part of the tyrant has been confirmed, the freemen opt to remain unorganized for fear of falling victim to the potential tyranny of any organization they themselves might create. This is the great downside to the American's spirit of independence: A lack of the innate camaraderie so commonly found amongst countrymen.

This leaves us confronting the conflicting nature of American politics. Its effects on the American militia movement, and like-minded organizations, are profound. Looking back, we see that those who founded our country banded together for a common cause, that of liberty. Yet after the War of Independence had been won they dispersed, creating not one nation, but a collection of independent states with a weak Federal government with, effectively, only the power to set foreign policy (which it was also nearly powerless to do, lacking an effective army and navy). While this governmental disorganization would be remedied somewhat by the Constitution, nothing has since been done to effectively organize the populace into armed groups with the purpose of preserving traditional American liberty.

This, the nature of American personality and politics, is my chief concern when it comes to the so-called "militia movement(s)." Many operate on extremely local levels. Using the current gun control situation in Virginia as an example we can see that, while local militias could be effective in the initial stages of any theoretical conflict, eventually they would be overpowered by the centrally-organized forces of the American state and Federal governments. This leaves the militia movement with three choices: 1) Create a centrally-organized chain of command, either on a state-by-state basis or at the national level; 2) Choose to avoid centralization altogether and instead opt to undertake fourth-dimensional warfare-esque operations in small cells of fifty men at most, as grassroots insurgents have done in decades past; 3) Or, finally, opt for a combination of the first two options, which will entail the creation of small guerrilla cells alongside a central command, to be used as a means toward attaining a formal government of their own (as the early IRA or Vietcong did).

The first option strikes me as theoretically ideal but practically impossible. It presents too many challenges, and many potential recruits would be troubled by the great potential for infiltration by FBI and the like, who, although unjustly, would take the formation of such a nation-wide militia as a threat to public safety. The individualistic spirit of many Americans, and the lack of true dedication to the cause of any "militia," will prevent the formation of any centralized militia organization. America's political climate is simply incapable of supporting such a group, especially in a time of relative prosperity like today.

The second option lacks any means toward proper, concrete ends. The proper ends for any American militia movement during any kind of future civil conflict, in my opinion, being the formation of a governmental body counter to the Federal or state governments. This third option provides militia movements the means to create an effective governing body and an armed force to back up its authority, as is necessary for any government. While bombastic, personality-driven American ideals will still guarantee that an anti-centralist faction remains within any militia-government, it will still be possible to create a government whose authority is respected and will help to lead the American people towards an intuitive, liberty-minded government.

Exploring Further the "Cowboy-Anarch" Archetype

The "Anarch" is one of many already well-established philosophical conceptions of an ideal man. In the words of Ernst Jünger, the concept's father, the "Anarch is not the partner of the monarch, but his antipode, the man that power cannot grasp but is also dangerous to it. He is not the adversary of the monarch, but his opposite." The Anarch is removed from society but is still able to observe it, separating himself as a means toward some higher end. Obviously

Jünger's Anarch concept, which originated in his 1977 dystopian novel "Eumeswil," remains valuable to metapolitical analyses of our society. This being said, I believe that the Anarch idea should be updated to better fit our times.

To understand more fully the whole of Jünger's philosophy, I should make mention of three other archetypes (or "characters") that appear in his literature. First there is the *Frontsoldat*, the "front soldier," whose personality is based upon Jünger's experiences during The Great War. From 1914 to 1918, Jünger witnessed the total transition not only of warfare, but also of society and its ideals, from pastoralism and romanticism towards technologization and industrialism. In the invention of new weapons such as machine guns, tanks and poison gas Jünger saw a profound transformation of humanity. Suddenly, life had taken on a machine-like character. Mass politics, mass warfare, mass industry: This new age ushered in by the war which engulfed Europe and much of the world in 1914 would be one defined by the masses, by numbers and machinery.

The second character is that of the Worker. The Worker, in Jünger's eyes, is tied to the soldier by the fact that both are children of this new age's technological, industrial spirit. The Worker, in this form, could be called a peacetime soldier. Jünger's Worker sought to bring the collective feelings of duty and fraternity found in soldierly life into the civilian world. The third of Jünger's archetype is the direct precursor to the Anarch, the Rebel. The Rebel has its roots in Jünger's relation to the Nazi regime and his 1939 book "On The Marble Cliffs," which describes the destruction of a peaceful rural, agricultural community by a despotic "head forester" and his followers. The book's message can either be interpreted as being anti-Nazi or anti-Stalinist, but either way its core message remains unchanged: It stood against totalitarianism of the masses. The Rebel is a freelancer because he fights not for any particular political system (he is alienated by them all), but simply for "freedom." Jünger writes, speaking of man's ultimate destruction by the world of mass politics: "The incredible encirclement of man was prepared long ago by the theories that aim at giving a flawless logical explanation of the world and that march in lockstep with the development of technology."

Having provided you a basic understanding of Jünger's philosophy, I can now begin to draw parallels between the original "Anarch" concept and its descendant, the "Cowboy-Anarch." It should be known that while the Cowboy-Anarch is inspired in part by Jünger's works, I am not claiming that Jünger would approve of it nor am I attempting to hijack the legacy of his literature/philosophy.

How does the concept of the Anarch remain relevant in its latest incarnation, the "Cowboy-Anarch?" Simply put, there are many individuals within our society that are unfulfilled or are seeking an escape from its mass-driven nature. We see this discontent manifested in numerous ways, from increased mental illness and dissociation to the rise of radical politics on both the right and left. The inevitable triumph of mass politics and technology over quiet, pastoral life has left a hole in the human psyche that has yet to be filled by any modern social or technological invention. While it is possible that, eventually, these malcontents will be placated by the natural course of social developments, it is not certain. Thus it will prove an important task to direct the destructive energies of youthful, discontented masses towards productive ends. This is the purpose of the Cowboy-Anarch ideal.

I draw upon the symbolism of America's Old West because it represents picturesque freedom: Beautiful nature, near-endless expanses of land on which to live, and isolation from cosmopolitan, bourgeois society. Who among you can say that this is not an appealing idea? The practicality of the Cowboy-Anarch ideal is another matter altogether.

Today, the acquisition of land and the means to provide for oneself and one's family is no small task. It goes without saying that this ideal is not within the reach of every man. This necessitates the adoption of certain surrogates that will enable every person to experience, at least partly, the life of a Cowboy-Anarch. While any activity that provides isolation from greater society is acceptable, I find that nature offers the greatest form of escape. Even if you are stuck in a classroom, an office, etc., for much of your time, I encourage you to put your free time to good use. Enjoy the liberating feeling of cold air, the serenity of a forest, and keep in your mind the ideal of self-reliance and freedom that the Cowboy Anarch symbolizes.

Conclusion

This document has laid out the groundwork for a new movement in American politics: the Cowboyist Party. Now that you have learned what it means to be a Cowboyist, I urge you to engage in activism within your local community. I will do the same in mine, always striving to improve the lives of those around me by any means possible. Prepare yourself for both hard and easy times, and never go a day without reflection. I will send you on your way with one simple message: Do no harm and embrace the less fortunate; remain principled and humble; go

forth and bring peace, strength, and diligence to
your community.

Yee-haw.

www.ingramcontent.com/pod-product-compliance
Lightning Source LLC
Chambersburg PA
CBHW051400280526
45784CB00007B/3038